Spanish-English Bilingual Short Stories for Kids

12 Easy 5-Minute Stories with Side-by-Side English and Spanish to Build First Words and Reading Confidence (Ages 4 to 6)

World Voice Bridge

Contents

Note to Parents

Dear Parent,

The fact that you are holding this book means you have already done something important. You chose to sit down, slow down, and share a story with your child. That decision matters more than you may realize. Research consistently shows that children who are read to regularly develop stronger language skills, wider vocabularies, and a deeper love of learning. But beyond the research, there is something simpler at work: your child will remember that you were there.

Reading at this age is not about speed. It is not about getting every word right or finishing a page without losing focus. It is about comfort, rhythm, and the feeling of finishing something all the way to the end. Every time you read with your child, you are teaching them that stories are worth staying with, and that they are capable of seeing something through.

This book contains twelve short stories, each one complete on its own. The children in these pages are ordinary kids in ordinary moments: a garden that needs watering, a coat with five stubborn buttons, a dark bedroom that feels too big at night. The problems are small. The emotions are familiar. Every story ends with a quiet moment of confidence that your child will feel right along with the characters.

You may notice repetition. That repetition is intentional. When children hear the same pattern more than once, they begin to anticipate it. When they anticipate it, they participate. When they participate, they grow. That is not just good storytelling. That is how young minds build the connections that turn listening into reading.

At the end of each story you will find four vocabulary words taken directly from the pages your child just heard. These are concrete, everyday words that can be seen, touched, and pointed to in real life. The simple fill-in activity is not meant to test your child. It is meant to build familiarity, one sound at a time. Celebrate every attempt. The effort is the point.

This edition is bilingual. Once you have read a story in English, try it again in Spanish, or let your child lead the way. Familiar words sound different in a new language, and that surprise is its own small lesson. You do not have to read both languages in the same sitting. Follow your child's energy and let the two versions find their own rhythm.

If your child asks to hear the same story again tomorrow, that is not a step backward. That is success. Repetition builds confidence. Confidence builds readers. And you, simply by being here, are building both.

STORY 1

Milo and the Missing Watering Can

English

Milo loved his garden.

Every morning, he pulled on his muddy boots and ran outside.

He had tomatoes by the fence.

He had tall sunflowers by the wall.

He had tiny carrot seeds in a neat little row.

Today was watering day.

Milo smiled.

He opened the gate.

And then he stopped.

His red watering can was missing.

Milo blinked.

He looked behind the big clay pot.

No watering can.

He looked under the wooden bench.

No watering can.

He put his hands on his hips.

"Where is my watering can?" he said.

He walked to the shed.

He moved the rake.

He looked behind a bag of soil.

He found a dusty glove.

He found two pinecones.

But no watering can.

"Where is my watering can?" he said again.

Milo felt worried.

His plants were thirsty.

Then he saw the garden hose near the gate.

Maybe the hose could help.

He turned the handle very slowly.

Water rushed out in a shiny arc.

Milo smiled.

He walked to the tomatoes.

Splash.

He walked to the sunflowers.

Splash.

He walked to the carrots.

Splash.

The water soaked into the soil.

The plants looked happy.

Milo felt proud.

Then he looked up.

And there it was.

His red watering can.

It was hanging on a hook by the fence.

Right where it always went.

Milo laughed.

"My watering can was not missing," he said.

"I just didn't see it."

He hung it neatly on its hook.

He gave his smallest tomato plant a gentle pat.

Then he went inside for breakfast.

His boots left muddy footprints on the floor.

But Milo did not notice.

He was still smiling.

Spanish

CUENTO 1: MILO Y LA REGADERA PERDIDA

Milo amaba su jardín.

Cada mañana corría apresurado con las botas llenas de barro.

Los tomates estaban al pie del cerco.

Los largos girasoles al pie de la pared.

Las semillitas de zanahoria en línea recta.

Hoy tocaba regar.

Milo sonrió.

Abrió el portón.

Y de repente paró.

Su regadera roja había desaparecido.

Milo parpadeó.

Buscó detrás del gran jarrón de arcilla.

No la encontró.

Buscó debajo del banco de madera.

No la encontró.

Descansó las manos en su cadera.

—¿Dónde está mi regadera? —se preguntó.

Se dirigió a la caseta.

Movió el rastrillo.

Buscó detrás de un saco de tierra.

Encontró un guante empolvado.

Encontró dos piñas de pino.

Pero no encontró su regadera.

—¿Dónde está mi regadera? —se preguntó nuevamente.

Milo se preocupó.

Sus plantas estaban sedientas.

Vio entonces la manguera, descansando cerca del cerco.

Quizás la manguera podría cooperar.

Muy despacito volteó el seguro de la manguera.

El agua brotó formando un brillante arco.

Milo sonrió.

Se dirigió hacia los tomates.

Plas.

Se dirigió hacia los girasoles.

Plas.

Se dirigió hacia las zanahorias.

Plas.

El agua desapareció dentro de la tierra.

Las plantas se veían felices.

Milo se enorgulleció.

Luego, levantó la mirada.

Ahí estaba ella.

Su regadera roja.

Colgaba de un gancho en el cerco.

En su lugar de siempre.

Milo rio.

—Mi regadera no se había perdido —dijo.

—Yo no la había visto.

La acomodó en el gancho cuidadosamente.

Le dio unas suaves palmaditas a su tomate más pequeñito.

Volvió a casa para desayunar.

Caminó dejando huellas de barro en el suelo.

Pero Milo no lo notó.

Una sonrisa en su rostro se dibujó.

Vocabulary

Illustration	English	Español
	TOMATO	TOMATE
	HOSE	MANGUERA
	GATE	PORTÓN
	CAN	REGADERA

Your Turn

Illustration	English	Español
	T_ _ _ _ _O	T_ _ _ _ _ _E
	H _ _ E	M_ _ _ _ _ _ _ A

Illustration	English	Español
	G _ _ E	P_ _ _ _ N
	C_ N	R_ _ _ _ _ _ A

STORY 2

Priya Makes Oatmeal

English

Priya woke up early on Saturday.

She had one big idea.

"I am going to make oatmeal all by myself," she said.

She had watched her grandmother many times.

You need a bowl.

You need a spoon.

You need oats.

Priya walked into the kitchen.

The oats were on the high shelf.

She climbed onto the step stool.

She stretched her arms up high.

She reached.

She almost touched the bag.

But not quite.

She stepped down.

"I can reach it," she said.

She climbed up again.

She stood on her tiptoes.

She stretched higher.

Still not enough.

"I can reach it," she said again.

Priya looked around.

She saw a thick wooden cutting board.

She had an idea.

She placed the cutting board flat on top of the stool.

She climbed up slowly.

She held the counter with both hands.

She reached up one more time.

This time, her fingers grabbed the bag of oats.

"Yes!" she whispered.

She climbed down carefully.

She found a bowl.

She found a spoon.

She scooped two spoonfuls of oats.

Then one tiny extra scoop.

She added water.

She put the bowl in the microwave.

She waited.

When it was ready, the oatmeal smelled warm and cozy.

Priya carried it to the table.

She added a little honey.

She took a bite.

It tasted just right.

Her grandmother walked into the kitchen.

She saw the bowl.

She saw the spoon.

She saw Priya smiling.

"You made oatmeal?" Grandma asked.

Priya nodded.

"All by myself," she said.

Grandma smiled.

Priya smiled back.

It was the best oatmeal she had ever tasted.

Spanish

CUENTO 2: LA AVENA QUE PREPARÓ PRIYA

Priya se despertó temprano el sábado.

Se le ocurrió una gran idea.

—Yo solita me voy a preparar un tazón de avena.

Muchas veces había observado a su abuela.

Necesitas un cuenco.

Necesitas una cuchara.

Necesitas avena.

Priya se dirigió a la cocina.

La avena estaba en la repisa alta.

Subió al banquillo.

Estiró los brazos tanto como pudo.

Se extendió.

Casi tocó la bolsa.

Casi, pero no lo logró.

Descendió.

—Yo puedo alcanzarla —se convenció.

Intentó subir nuevamente.

Se paró de puntillas.

Se estiró aún más.

«Casi» no era suficiente.

—Yo puedo alcanzarla —se repitió.

Priya miró a su alrededor.

Observó una gruesa tabla de picar de madera.

Se le ocurrió una idea.

Colocó la tabla de picar encima del banquillo.

Subió despacito.

Puso ambas manos sobre la barra.

Se estiró una vez más.

Esta vez sus dedos alcanzaron la bolsa de avena.

—¡Sí! —susurró.

Bajó del banquillo cuidadosamente.

Encontró un cuenco.

Encontró una cuchara.

Contó dos cucharadas llenas de avena.

Y luego una cucharada pequeñísima extra.

Añadió agua.

Metió el cuenco en el microondas.

Esperó.

Una vez lista, la avena olía cálida y acogedora.

Priya lo llevó a la mesa.

Añadió un poquito de miel.

Comió un poquito.

El sabor era perfecto.

Su abuela entró a la cocina.

Observó el cuenco.

Observó la cuchara.

Observó la sonrisa de Priya.

—¿Preparaste avena? —preguntó.

Priya asintió.

—Yo solita —respondió.

Su abuela sonrió.

Priya le devolvió la sonrisa.

Era la mejor avena que había probado.

Vocabulary

Illustration	English	Español
	OATS	AVENA
	SPOON	CUCHARA
	BOWL	CUENCO
	STOOL	BANQUILLO

Your Turn

Illustration	English	Español
	O_ _ S	A_ _ _ A

Illustration	English	Español
	S _ _ _ N	C_ _ _ _ _ A
	B_ _ L	C_ _ _ _O
	S _ _ _ L	B_ _ _ _ _ _ _ O

STORY 3

Otto and the Lost Bucket

English

Otto ran onto Pelican Shore.

He had a big plan.

"I am going to build the tallest sandcastle ever," he said.

He opened the beach bag.

He pulled out his towel.

He pulled out his sunscreen.

He pulled out his water bottle.

Then he stopped.

His bucket was missing.

Otto blinked.

He looked inside the bag again.

Goggles.

Crackers.

A book for Mom.

No bucket.

"My bucket has to be here," Otto said.

He shook the bag.

He checked every pocket.

Still no bucket.

"My bucket has to be here," he said again.

He ran to the car.

He looked in the back seat.

He looked under the seat.

He saw a sock.

He saw a juice box.

No bucket.

Otto walked back to the sand.

The waves splashed over his toes.

He felt a little sad.

"I cannot build the tallest sandcastle without my bucket," he said.

Just then, a wave rolled in.

When it rolled back out, it left something behind.

Otto ran forward.

It was a big white shell.

It was smooth and curved like a tiny bowl.

Otto held it in his hands.

He thought for a moment.

Then he smiled.

He scooped sand with the shell.

It worked.

He packed the sand with his hands.

He smoothed the walls.

He scooped.

He packed.

He patted.

He worked and worked.

Soon, he had a wide, strong sandcastle.

It had three little rooms.

It had a moat that was filled with water.

Mom walked over and shaded her eyes.

"Otto," she said, "did you build that without your bucket?"

Otto held up the shell.

"My bucket was lost," he said.

"But I found something else."

Mom smiled.

Otto smiled back.

It was not the tallest sandcastle ever.

But it was the best one he had ever made.

Spanish

CUENTO 3: OTTO Y LA CUBETA PERDIDA

Otto se apresuró para llegar a la playa Pelican Shore.

Tenía un gran plan.

—Voy a construir el castillo de arena más alto del mundo —decidió.

Abrió la bolsa de playa.

Sacó su toalla.

Sacó su protector solar.

Sacó su botella de agua.

De repente, se detuvo.

Faltaba su cubeta.

Otto pestañeó.

Sus ojos examinaron la bolsa nuevamente.

Lentes de natación.

Galletas.

Un libro para mamá.

No estaba su cubeta.

—Mi cubeta tiene que estar acá —declaró Otto.

Le dio un sacudón a la bolsa.

Buscó en cada bolsillo.

No estaba su cubeta.

—Mi cubeta tiene que estar acá —se repitió.

Corrió al auto.

Examinó el asiento trasero.

Examinó debajo del asiento.

Encontró una media.

Encontró un jugo en caja.

Pero no su cubeta.

Otto caminó hasta la arena.

Las olas le tocaron los pies.

Se sintió un poquito triste.

—No puedo construir el castillo de arena más alto del mundo sin mi cubeta —exclamó.

De pronto, una ola se acercó.

Al alejarse, algo dejó.

Otto corrió.

Era una gran concha marina de color blanco.

Su superficie era lisa y curva como un cuenco pequeño.

Otto la sostuvo en sus manos.

Se tomó un momento para pensar.

Luego sonrió.

Levantó la arena con la concha.

Funcionó.

Comprimió la arena con las manos.

Alisó las paredes.

Levantó.

Comprimió.

Alisó.

Se esforzó muchísimo.

En poco tiempo había construido un castillo de arena amplio y sólido.

Contaba con tres habitaciones pequeñas.

Tenía también una pequeña fosa repleta de agua.

Su mamá se acercó y se cubrió del sol con las manos.

—Otto... ¿construiste esto sin tu cubeta? —preguntó.

Otto sostuvo su concha marina en alto.

—Perdí mi cubeta —respondió.

—Pero encontré esto.

Su mamá sonrió.

Otto le devolvió la sonrisa.

No era el castillo de arena más grande del mundo.

Pero era el mejor castillo que había construido.

Vocabulary

Illustration	English	Español
	BUCKET	CUBETA
	WAVE	OLA
	SHELL	CONCHA
	SAND	ARENA

Your Turn

Illustration	English	Español
	B _ _ _ _ T	C _ _ _ _ A

Illustration	English	Español
	W _ _ E	O_A
	S _ _ _ L	C _ _ _ _ A
	S _ _ D	A_ _ _ A

STORY 4

Lena and the Lamp

English

Lena loved rainy Saturdays.

She loved the library best when rain tapped the tall windows.

Tap. Tap. Tap.

She found her favorite desk in the corner.

The desk had a little lamp with a green shade.

Lena opened her book.

She started to read.

Then the lamp flickered.

Blink.

Blink.

Dark.

Lena looked at the lamp.

"Oh no," she whispered.

She pressed the button.

Nothing.

She pressed it again.

Still nothing.

"My lamp," she said softly.

She looked at the pages.

They were too dark.

"I need my lamp," she said.

Lena carried her book to the window.

Gray light came through the glass.

She held her book up high.

She read one page.

Then two.

A big truck splashed water on the window.

The room grew darker.

"I need my lamp," Lena said again.

She walked slowly to the front desk.

A librarian with shiny silver earrings smiled at her.

"Is something wrong?" the librarian asked.

"My lamp went dark," Lena said.

The librarian nodded.

"Let's find you some light."

She brought a small lamp and a long cord.

They plugged it in at Lena's desk.

Click.

Warm yellow light filled the corner.

Lena smiled.

"My lamp is back," she said.

She curled up in her chair.

She read and read.

The fox in her story made it home before the snow.

Outside, the rain kept tapping.

Inside, Lena's lamp glowed warm and bright.

It was the perfect rainy day.

Spanish

CUENTO 4: LENA Y LA LÁMPARA

Lena amaba los sábados lluviosos.

Los días que disfrutaba más la biblioteca eran los mismos en los que la lluvia golpeaba las ventanas altas.

Plic. Plic. Plic.

Ubicó su escritorio favorito en una esquina.

El escritorio tenía una pequeña lámpara verde.

Lena abrió su libro.

Empezó a leer.

La lámpara parpadeó.

Blink.

Blink.

Oscuridad.

Lena observó la lámpara.

—Oh no —susurró.

Presionó el botón.

Nada.

Lo presionó nuevamente.

Nada.

—Mi lámpara —dijo suavemente.

Dirigió su atención a las páginas.

Se veían muy oscuras.

—Necesito mi lámpara —declaró.

Lena caminó con su libro a la ventana.

La luz gris atravesó el vidrio.

Sostuvo su libro a la altura de su vista.

Leyó la primera página.

Luego la segunda.

Un gran camión salpicó agua a la ventana al pasar.

La sala se oscureció aún más.

—Necesito mi lámpara —dijo nuevamente.

Se dirigió lentamente a la recepción.

Una bibliotecaria de aretes plateados y brillosos le sonrió.

—¿Pasa algo? —preguntó la bibliotecaria.

—Mi lámpara no prende — respondió Lena.

La bibliotecaria asintió.

—Déjame ayudarte para que tengas luz.

Trajo una pequeña lámpara y un cable largo.

La conectó y la puso sobre el escritorio de Lena.

Clic.

La esquina se iluminó con una luz cálida y amarilla.

Lena sonrió.

—Tengo una lámpara de nuevo—dijo.

Se acomodó en su asiento.

Leyó y continuó leyendo.

El zorro de la historia llegó a casa antes de que nevara.

En el exterior, las gotas de lluvia seguían golpeando las ventanas.

En el interior, la lámpara de Lena brillaba cálida y radiante.

Era el día lluvioso perfecto.

Vocabulary

Illustration	English	Español
	BOOK	LIBRO

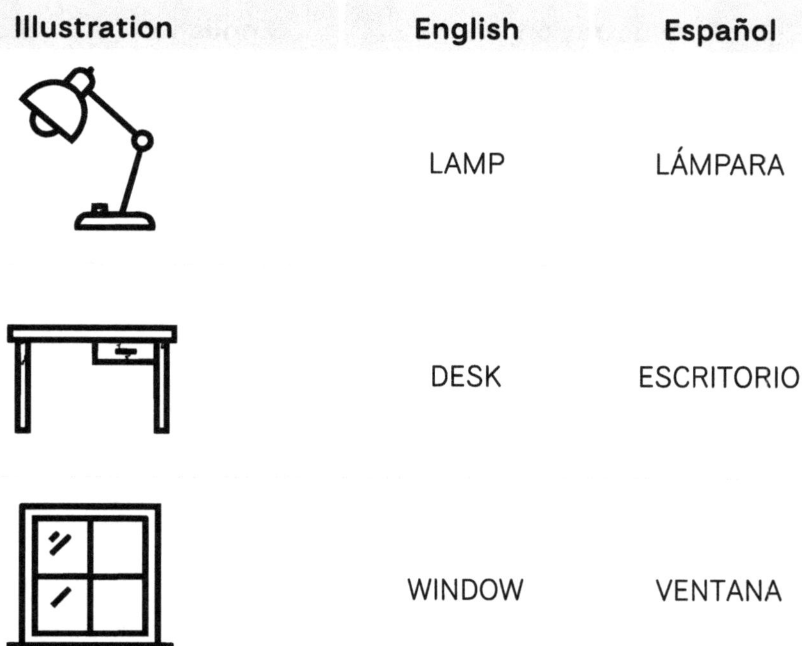

Illustration	English	Español
	LAMP	LÁMPARA
	DESK	ESCRITORIO
	WINDOW	VENTANA

Your Turn

Illustration	English	Español
	B _ _ K	L _ _ _ O
	L _ _ P	L _ _ _ _ _ A
	D _ _ K	E _ _ _ _ _ _ _ _ _ O

Illustration	English	Español
	W _ _ _ _ W	V _ _ _ _ _A

A Little Thank-You Gift for You and Your Little Reader

If you're reading this book alongside your child, I want to thank you from the heart. Your decision to make reading part of your daily routine is more than a habit; it's a step toward building your child's confidence, giving them the gift of two languages, and creating moments together they will carry for the rest of their lives.

Because learning should feel simple, playful, and full of joy, I've created two special bonus materials to help your child go even further and make your job as their reading partner a little easier.

Here's What You'll Get (For Free!)

Bonus One: Free 40-Page Bilingual Activity Workbook Hands-on English and Spanish activities your child can do right after storytime.

- Drawing and activity pages, tracing sheets, and matching games for little ones ages 4 to 6
- Writing prompts, word challenges, and vocabulary activities for growing readers ages 6 to 8
- Every page is fully bilingual so your child practices both languages while having fun

Bonus Two: Parent Guide: How to Raise a Bilingual Reader Everything you need to turn 15 minutes a day into a lifelong love of two languages.

- A simple weekly reading schedule designed around real family life
- How to alternate languages, when to repeat stories, and how to make vocabulary stick
- The most common mistakes parents make when teaching two languages and how to avoid every one of them

These free bonuses are here to support your child, encourage their curiosity, and remind you that raising a bilingual reader can be simple and deeply rewarding every single day.

How to Access Your Free Bonuses: Scan the QR code below to unlock your materials instantly.

Gracias de corazon, thank you from the heart, for choosing to share these stories with your child.

You're not just reading a book together. You're building the foundation of who they will become.

Keep going. You've got this.

With appreciation, World Voice Bridge

STORY 5

Theo's Loud Morning

English

Theo loved his grandparents' farm.

He loved the cows.

He loved the barn.

He loved the wide, open fields.

But he did not love the rooster.

The rooster's name was Gerald.

Gerald was very loud.

Every morning, Gerald crowed.

"COCK-A-DOODLE-DOO!"

It was always loud.

It was always sudden.

It was always Theo's loud morning.

On Thursday, Grandpa said, "Theo, can you bring some hay to the barn?"

Theo put on his boots.

He stood at the kitchen door.

He looked across the yard.

Gerald was out there somewhere.

Theo swallowed.

"I am not afraid," he whispered.

He stepped outside.

The grass was wet.

The air was cool.

Theo walked slowly.

Step.

Step.

Step.

He reached the barn.

He scooped up a big armful of hay.

Then,

"COCK-A-DOODLE-DOO!"

Theo jumped.

Hay fell to the ground.

Gerald was standing right behind him.

Theo's heart thumped fast.

Gerald blinked.

Theo took a deep breath.

He stood up straight.

"This is my loud morning," Theo said.

"And I am not afraid."

Gerald blinked again.

Then he made a tiny cluck.

Theo picked up the hay.

He walked past Gerald.

He spread the hay inside the fence.

Gerald stayed where he was.

Quiet.

Theo walked back to the house.

Grandpa smiled.

"How was your morning?" Grandpa asked.

Theo smiled back.

"It was loud," he said.

"But I was brave."

And that made it a very good morning.

Spanish

CUENTO 5: LA MAÑANA RUIDOSA DE THEO

Theo amaba la granja de sus abuelos.

Amaba las vacas.

Amaba el granero.

Amaba el campo, libre y amplio.

Si había algo que no amaba, era al gallo.

Su nombre era Gerald.

Gerald hacía muchísimo ruido.

No había mañana en la que Gerald no cantara.

—¡QUIQUIRIQUÍ!

Siempre a todo pulmón.

Siempre inesperado.

Todas las mañanas eran ruidosas para Theo.

—Theo, ¿puedes traer un poco de heno del granero? —le pidió el día jueves su abuelo.

Theo se colocó sus botas.

Se detuvo en la puerta de la cocina.

Examinó el patio.

En algún lugar debía estar Gerald.

Theo pasó saliva.

—No tengo miedo —susurró.

Puso un pie afuera.

El césped estaba húmedo.

El aire estaba fresco.

Theo caminó lentamente.

Tap.

Tap.

Tap.

Llegó al granero.

Levantó en brazos mucho heno.

De repente,

—¡QUIQUIRIQUÍ!

Theo pegó un brinco.

El heno cayó al piso.

Gerald se erguía a sus espaldas.

El corazón de Theo empezó a latir rápidamente.

Gerald parpadeó.

Theo suspiró profundamente.

Se puso firme.

—Es mi mañana ruidosa —declaró Theo.

—No tengo miedo.

Gerald parpadeó nuevamente.

Después, soltó un breve «co».

Theo levantó el heno.

Pasó por un costado de Gerald.

Dispersó el heno dentro de la valla.

Gerald permaneció en el mismo lugar.

Quieto.

Theo volvió a casa.

Su abuelo sonrió.

—¿Qué me cuentas sobre tu mañana? —preguntó su abuelo.

Theo le devolvió la sonrisa.

—Fue ruidosa —respondió.

—Pero fui valiente —añadió.

Y eso la convirtió en una buena mañana.

Vocabulary

Illustration	English	Español
	BARN	GRANERO

Illustration	English	Español
	ROOSTER	GALLO
	HAY	HENO
	BOOTS	BOTAS

Your Turn

Illustration	English	Español
	B _ _ N	G_ _ _ _ _ _O
	R _ _ _ _ _ _ R	G_ _ _O
	H _ Y	H_ _O

Illustration	English	Español
	B _ _ _ S	B_ _ _S

STORY 6

Nadia Waits

English

Nadia ran into the playground.

She saw the swing.

It was the best swing.

It had long chains.

It went very, very high.

But someone was already on it.

A boy with red mittens was swinging.

Higher.

Higher.

Higher.

Nadia stopped.

She felt a tight feeling in her chest.

She wanted that swing.

She looked at her mom on the bench.

Mom gave her a small smile.

Nadia took a deep breath.

"I can wait," she whispered.

She walked to the slide.

Whoosh!

Down she went.

She climbed up again.

Whoosh!

Down again.

She stopped and looked.

The boy was still swinging.

Nadia crossed her arms.

Then she uncrossed them.

"I can wait," she said again.

She went to the rope ladder.

It wobbled.

She climbed up.

Step.

Step.

Step.

She touched the top.

She climbed down.

She looked at the swing.

Still taken.

"I can wait," she said softly.

She climbed the rope ladder again.

And again.

Then she heard footsteps.

The boy with red mittens hopped off the swing.

He ran toward the water fountain.

Nadia's eyes grew wide.

She hurried to the swing.

She grabbed the chains.

She sat down.

She pushed with her feet.

Back and forth.

Higher.

Higher.

Higher.

The wind rushed past her ears.

Her hair flew behind her.

Mom waved from the bench.

Nadia waved back.

"I waited," she said proudly.

And it was worth it.

Spanish

CUENTO 6: LA ESPERA DE NADIA

Nadia corrió hacia el patio de juegos.

Ubicó el columpio.

Era el mejor columpio.

Tenía las cadenas más largas.

Y llegaba muy, pero muy alto.

Pero ya había alguien sentado ahí.

Un niño con guantecitos rojos se columpiaba.

Más alto.

Más alto.

Más alto.

Nadia se detuvo.

Se le apachurró el corazón.

Ella quería subirse al columpio.

Miró a su mamá sentada en el banco.

Su mamá le lanzó una sonrisita.

Nadia suspiró profundamente.

—Puedo esperar —susurró.

Caminó hacia el tobogán.

¡Wuush!

Se deslizó.

Volvió a subir.

¡Wuush!

Se deslizó nuevamente.

Se detuvo a mirar.

El niño seguía columpiándose.

Nadia se cruzó de brazos.

Luego los dejó caer a cada lado.

—Puedo esperar —se repitió a sí misma.

Fue hacia la escalera de cuerda.

Se tambaleó.

Escaló.

Paso.

Paso.

Paso.

Llegó a la cima.

Emprendió su descenso.

Miró el columpio.

Él aún estaba ahí.

—Puedo esperar —se dijo suavemente.

Volvió a escalar la escalera de cuerda.

Y volvió a subir.

Luego, escuchó pasos.

El niño de los guantecitos rojos se había bajado del columpio.

Se dirigía hacia la fuente de agua.

Los ojos de Nadia crecieron.

Se apresuró para llegar al columpio.

Agarró las cadenas.

Se sentó.

Se impulsó con los pies.

De atrás hacia adelante.

Más alto.

Más alto.

Más alto.

El aire se apresuraba tras sus oídos.

Su cabello ondeaba tras ella.

Su mamá la saludó con la mano.

Nadia le devolvió el saludo.

—Esperé —dijo orgullosa.

Valió la pena.

Vocabulary

Illustration	English	Español
	SWING	COLUMPIO
	SLIDE	TOBOGÁN
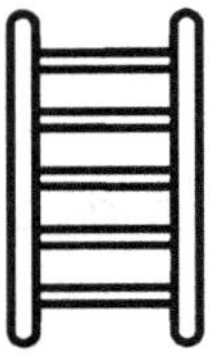	LADDER	ESCALERA
	ROPE	CUERDA

Your Turn

Illustration	English	Español
	S _ _ _ G	C_ _ _ _ _ _ _ O
	S _ _ _ E	T_ _ _ _ _ _N

Illustration	English	Español
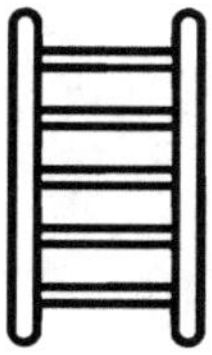	L _ _ _ _ R	E_ _ _ _ _ _ _ A
	R _ _ E	C_ _ _ _A

Change Lives with Your Review

Share the Gift of Reading

"One language sets you in a corridor for life. Two languages open every door along the way."
— Frank Smith, Psycholinguist

Parents who invest in their children's growth tend to raise more confident, curious, and connected kids. Let's team up to make a difference!

Can you lend a hand to someone just like you, a parent who wants the best for their child but is not sure where to start with bilingual reading?

My goal is to make raising a bilingual reader feel simple, joyful, and totally possible for every family.

To spread the word, I need your support.

Most parents choose books because of reviews from other parents. So I am asking you, a fellow family builder, to leave a quick and honest review.

It is free, takes less than a minute, and your honest words could change the direction of a child's life. If this book made a difference in your home, your honest words might...

- Give one more child the gift of two languages before they start school.
- Help one more parent feel confident reading with their child every night.
- Show one more family that 15 minutes a day is enough to make a real difference.
- Connect one more child to their culture, their heritage, and their voice.
- Turn one more bedtime story into a lifelong love of reading.

To help out, just scan the QR code below and drop a review:

[https://www.amazon.com/review/review-your-purchases/?asin=BOOKASIN]

If you believe every child deserves the chance to grow up hearing two languages, we are kindred spirits. Thank you so much from the bottom of my heart!

World Voice Bridge

STORY 7

Felix and the Dark

English

Felix did not like the dark.

When the lights went off, his room felt very big.

The house got quiet.

Very quiet.

Felix lay on his pillow.

He pulled his blanket up to his chin.

"I don't like the dark," he whispered.

On Tuesday night, he called for Dad.

Dad came and sat on the edge of the bed.

The mattress dipped down in a cozy way.

"I can't sleep," Felix said. "It's too dark."

Dad did not turn on the light.

Instead, he said, "Let's listen."

"To what?" Felix asked.

"To the dark," Dad said.

Felix listened.

He heard the clock in the hallway.

Tick.

Tick.

Tick.

He had never noticed it before.

Dad smiled.

"The dark has sounds," he said softly.

Then Dad hugged Felix and left the room.

Felix listened again.

He heard the wind outside.

Whooo.

Whooo.

It was the pine tree moving.

He looked at his window.

He saw three tiny stars.

They were small.

They were steady.

They did not move.

Felix took a deep breath.

"The dark is not empty," he whispered.

"It has the clock. It has the wind. It has the stars."

He pulled the blanket tighter.

Tick.

Whooo.

Shine.

The dark did not feel so big anymore.

Felix closed his eyes.

Soon, he was asleep.

In the morning, he told Dad.

"I listened to the dark," Felix said.

Dad smiled.

"And what did you hear?"

Felix grinned.

"Everything."

Spanish

CUENTO 7: FELIX Y LA OSCURIDAD

A Felix no le gustaba la oscuridad.

Su habitación se sentía inmensa cuando se apagaban las luces.

La casa se llenaba de silencio.

Mucho silencio.

Felix recostó su cabeza en su almohada.

Se cubrió con la cobija hasta el mentón.

—No me gusta la oscuridad —susurró.

La noche del martes, llamó a su papá.

Su papá se acercó y se sentó al borde de la cama.

El colchón se hundió gratamente.

—No puedo dormir —dijo—. Está muy oscuro.

Pero su papá no prendió la luz.

—Escuchemos.

—¿Escuchar qué? —preguntó.

—A la oscuridad —respondió su papá.

Felix escuchó.

Escuchó cómo sonaba el reloj del pasadizo.

Tic tac.

Tic tac.

Tic tac.

Nunca lo había notado.

Su papá sonrió.

—La oscuridad suena —dijo suavemente.

Entonces lo abrazó y salió de su habitación.

Felix volvió a escuchar.

Escuchó el viento que sonaba afuera.

Wuush.

Wuush.

Ese era el pino moviéndose.

Observó su ventana.

Vio tres estrellitas.

Eran muy pequeñitas.

Permanecían fijas.

No se movían.

Felix respiró hondo.

—La oscuridad no está vacía —susurró.

—Tiene al reloj, al viento y a las estrellas —dijo.

Se arropó más con la cobija.

Tic tac.

Wuush.

Luz.

La oscuridad ya no se sentía tan inmensa.

Felix cerró los ojos.

Se durmió muy poco después.

En la mañana, le contó a su papá.

—Escuché lo que tenía que decir la oscuridad —dijo Felix.

Su papá sonrió.

—¿Y qué escuchaste? —preguntó.

Felix sonrió ampliamente.

—De todo —dijo.

Vocabulary

Illustration	English	Español
	CLOCK	RELOJ
	BLANKET	COBIJA
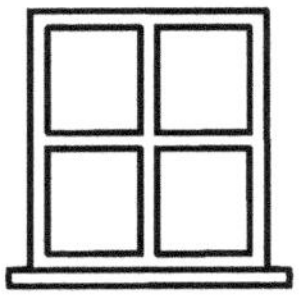	WINDOW	VENTANA
	STAR	ESTRELLA

Your Turn

Illustration	English	Español
	C _ _ _ K	R _ _ _J
	B _ _ _ _ _ _ T	C_ _ _ _A

Illustration	English	Español
	W _ _ _ _ W	V_ _ _ _ _ _ A
	S _ _ R	E_ _ _ _ _ _ _A

STORY 8

Rosa's Cookie

English

Rosa loved her aunt's bakery.

It had a yellow awning.

It smelled like sugar and butter.

Today was special.

Rosa was going to decorate a cookie.

Her aunt tied a small apron around her.

She showed Rosa the icing tube.

"Press gently," Aunt said.

"Stop before it runs off."

Rosa picked up a round sugar cookie.

She squeezed the icing.

Slow.

Slow.

She stopped at the edge.

It was perfect.

Rosa smiled.

"That is my cookie," she said proudly.

She reached for another one.

But her elbow bumped the tray.

Six cookies slid off.

Plop.

Plop.

Plop.

They broke on the floor.

Rosa froze.

Her face felt hot.

"I ruined them," she whispered.

Her aunt knelt down.

"You made a mistake," Aunt said softly.

"There is more dough."

Rosa helped clean up.

She washed her hands.

She watched Aunt roll out new dough.

Six new cookies went into the oven.

While they baked, Rosa practiced squeezing icing onto paper.

Slow.

Slow.

Stop.

The cookies came out warm.

They cooled on the tray.

Rosa picked up one.

"This one is mine," she said.

She pressed the icing slowly.

She stopped at the edge.

She added tiny colored dots.

Red.

Blue.

Yellow.

It was not perfect.

But it was hers.

Her aunt held it up.

"Rosa's cookie goes in the front window," Aunt said.

Rosa smiled.

The hot, prickly feeling was gone.

Now she felt warm inside.

She hung up her apron.

And she looked at her cookie shining in the window.

Spanish

CUENTO 8: La galleta de Rosa

Rosa amaba la pastelería de su tía.

Tenía un toldo amarillo.

Olía a azúcar y a mantequilla.

El día de hoy era especial.

Rosa decoraría una galleta.

Su tía le amarró un pequeño delantal a la cintura.

Le mostró a Rosa la manga pastelera.

—Aprieta suave —le indicó su tía.

—Suelta antes de que se acabe —añadió.

Rosa escogió una galleta redonda de azúcar.

Apretó la manga para que el glaseado saliera.

Lentamente.

Lentamente.

Se detuvo cuando llegó al borde.

Se veía perfecta.

Rosa sonrió.

—Es mi galleta —dijo con orgullo.

Estiró la mano para alcanzar otra.

Pero su codo golpeó la bandeja.

Seis galletas se deslizaron de esta.

Pof.

Pof.

Pof.

Se quebraron cuando golpearon el piso.

Rosa se congeló.

Sentía que su rostro hervía.

—Las arruiné —susurró.

Su tía se arrodilló.

—Cometiste un error —dijo su tía suavemente.

—Tenemos más masa —dijo.

Rosa le ayudó a limpiar.

Se lavó las manos.

Observó cómo su tía preparaba masa fresca.

Seis galletas nuevas ingresaron al horno.

Mientras se horneaban, Rosa practicaba en un papel cuánto glaseado usar.

Lentamente.

Lentamente.

Detenerse.

Las galletas estaban calientes.

Se enfriaron en la bandeja.

Rosa tomó una.

—Esta es mía —declaró.

Apretó lentamente la manga pastelera.

Se detuvo en el borde.

Las decoró con puntitos de colores.

Rojo.

Azul.

Amarillo.

No era perfecta.

Pero era suya.

Su tía la sostuvo.

—La galleta de Rosa va en el mostrador frontal —dijo su tía.

Rosa sonrió.

El sentimiento vergonzoso y punzante había desaparecido.

Ahora sentía calidez.

Colgó su delantal.

Y observó su galleta brillando en el mostrador.

Vocabulary

Illustration	English	Español
	COOKIE	GALLETA
	ICING	GLASEADO
	APRON	DELANTAL
	OVEN	HORNO

Your Turn

Illustration	English	Español
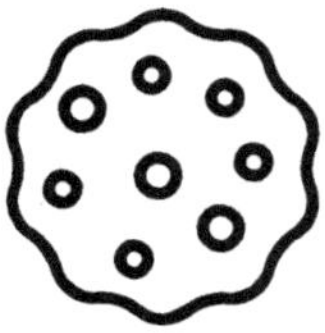	C _ _ _ _ E	G _ _ _ _ _ A
	I _ _ _ G	G _ _ _ _ _ _ O

Illustration	English	Español
	 A _ _ _ N	D_ _ _ _ _ _ _L
	O _ _ N	H_ _ _O

STORY 9

Sam and the Ducks

English

Sam went to Willowmere Pond.

He had a bag of bread crusts.

He was excited.

"I will feed the ducks," he said.

Then he saw them.

The ducks were big.

They paddled toward him.

Splash.

Splash.

Splash.

Sam stepped back.

His sneakers crunched on the reeds.

The ducks kept coming.

Their orange feet moved fast under the water.

Sam swallowed.

"They look bigger this year," he said.

His sister stood beside him.

She held out her hand.

"One small step," she said.

Sam took a breath.

"One small step," he whispered.

He moved closer to the water.

He pulled out one tiny crust.

He tossed it.

Plop.

Three ducks rushed to it.

Splash!

Sam jumped.

Then he laughed.

He tossed another crust.

Plop.

A duck with a shiny green head grabbed it.

Sam smiled.

"One small step," he said again.

He stepped closer.

He tossed another crust.

Plop.

Soon, Sam was standing at the edge of the pond.

The ducks made soft, happy sounds.

Quack.

Dip.

Splash.

Sam crouched down.

He held one crust flat on his hand.

The green-headed duck swam closer.

Closer.

Closer.

Sam held very still.

The duck took the bread.

Quick.

Gentle.

Sam blinked.

He laughed.

"I fed the ducks!" he said.

His sister smiled.

Sam sat by the water and fed the rest of the bread.

The ducks splashed and quacked.

Sam was not scared anymore.

He was brave.

And he had taken one small step at a time.

Spanish

CUENTO 9: Sam y los patos

Sam fue a visitar la laguna Willowmere Pond.

Llevaba consigo una bolsa de cortezas de pan.

Se sentía emocionado.

—Alimentaré a los patos —dijo.

Entonces los vio.

Los patos eran grandes.

Chapotearon hacia él.

Splash.

Splash.

Splash.

Sam retrocedió.

Sus zapatillas crujieron sobre los juncos.

Los patos seguían acercándose.

Sus patas naranjas se movían más rápido bajo el agua.

Sam pasó saliva.

—Este año parecen más grandes —dijo.

Su hermana permaneció de pie a su lado.

Ella extendió la mano.

—Un paso pequeño a la vez —dijo.

Sam respiró hondo.

—Un paso pequeño a la vez —respondió susurrando.

Se acercó al agua.

Sacó una pequeña corteza de pan.

La arrojó.

Plop.

Tres patos corrieron hacia ella.

¡Splash!

Sam pegó un brinco.

Luego, rio.

Lanzó otra corteza de pan.

Plop.

Se lo comió un pato que tenía la cabeza de color verde brillante.

Sam sonrió.

—Un paso pequeño a la vez —se repitió a sí mismo.

Se acercó.

Lanzó otra corteza.

Plop.

Muy pronto Sam estaba de pie al borde de la laguna.

Los patos hacían sonidos suaves y felices.

Cuac.

Dip.

Splash.

Sam se agachó.

Colocó una corteza de pan en la palma de su mano.

El pato que tenía la cabeza de color verde brillante se acercó nadando.

Cada vez más cerca.

Cada vez más cerca.

Sam no se movió.

El pato tomó el pan.

Rápidamente.

Gentilmente.

Sam parpadeó.

Rio.

—¡Alimenté a los patos! —dijo.

Su hermana sonrió.

Sam se sentó cerca al agua y alimentó con pan al resto.

Los patos salpicaban y graznaban.

Sam ya no tenía miedo.

Fue valiente.

Y había avanzado un pequeño paso a la vez.

Vocabulary

Illustration	English	Español
	DUCK	PATO
	POND	LAGUNA
	BREAD	PAN
	SNEAKERS	ZAPATILLAS

Your Turn

Illustration	English	Español
	D _ _ K	P_ _O
	P _ _ D	L_ _ _ _A

Illustration	English	Español
	 B _ _ _ D	P_N
	S _ _ _ _ _ _ S	Z_ _ _ _ _ _ _ _S

STORY 10

Ivy Buttons Up

English

Ivy's class was going on a nature walk.

Everyone grabbed their coats.

The coats hung on hooks in the hallway.

Ivy's hook had a blue butterfly.

She pulled down her coat.

She put her arms in the sleeves.

So far, so good.

Then she looked at the buttons.

There were five of them.

Round.

Brown.

Slippery.

Ivy tried the first button.

Push.

Wiggle.

Pop.

It went in.

She smiled.

She tried the second button.

Push.

Wiggle.

Oh no.

The first one slipped out.

Ivy made a tiny growl.

Her class was lining up at the door.

She felt her cheeks grow warm.

"Slow hands," she whispered.

"Slow hands."

She started at the bottom button.

Push.

Wait.

She felt it catch.

Good.

"Slow hands," she said again.

She moved to the next button.

Push.

Wait.

Catch.

She did not rush.

One button at a time.

Push.

Wait.

Catch.

By the fourth button, her fingers felt steady.

Push.

Wait.

Catch.

She pressed the last button through.

Then she smoothed her coat flat.

"Ivy buttons up," she said proudly.

Her teacher smiled from the doorway.

Outside, the air felt cool and fresh.

Ivy's coat stayed closed.

She found a red leaf.

She found a small acorn.

She found a soft gray feather.

Her coat stayed buttoned the whole walk.

Ivy walked tall.

She had done it herself.

Slow hands.

One button at a time.

Spanish

CUENTO 10: IVY ESTÁ ABOTONADA

La clase de Ivy iría a un paseo por la naturaleza.

Todos llevaban sus abrigos.

Los abrigos colgaban de ganchos en el pasadizo.

El gancho de Ivy tenía una mariposa azul.

Descolgó su abrigo.

Deslizó sus brazos por las mangas.

Todo iba bien.

Luego observó los botones.

Había cinco.

Redondos.

Marrones.

Resbalosos.

Ivy intentó abotonar el primer botón.

Empujó.

Movió.

Pop.

Encajó.

Sonrió.

Intentó abotonar el segundo botón.

Empujó.

Movió.

Oh no.

El primero se había desabotonado.

Ivy gruñó bajito.

Su clase se estaba formando en una fila en la puerta.

Sentía que sus mejillas se calentaban.

—Manos lentas —susurró.

—Manos lentas —se repitió.

Empezó por el último botón.

Empujó.

Esperó.

Sintió que encajó.

Bien.

—Manos lentas —se repitió.

Siguió con el siguiente botón.

Empujó.

Esperó.

Encajó.

No se apresuró.

Un botón a la vez.

Empujó.

Esperó.

Encajó.

Sus manos se sentían más estables al llegar al cuarto botón.

Empujó.

Esperó.

Encajó.

Empujó el último botón.

Alisó su abrigo con las manos.

—Ivy está toda abotonada —dijo orgullosa.

Su profesora le sonrió desde la puerta.

El aire del exterior era frío y fresco.

El abrigo de Ivy permaneció abotonado.

Encontró una hoja roja.

Encontró una pequeña bellota.

Encontró una pluma gris y suave.

El abrigo de Ivy permaneció abotonado todo el camino.

Ivy caminó erguida.

Lo había logrado ella sola.

Manos lentas.

Un botón a la vez.

Vocabulary

Illustration	English	Español
	COAT	ABRIGO
	BUTTON	BOTÓN
	HOOK	GANCHO
	BUTTERFLY	MARIPOSA

Your Turn

Illustration	English	Español
	C _ _ T	A_ _ _ _O

Illustration	English	Español
	B _ _ _ _ N	B_ _ _N
	H _ _ K	G_ _ _ _O
	B _ _ _ _ _ _ _ Y	M_ _ _ _ _ _A

STORY 11

Benny's Treehouse

English

Benny loved his treehouse.

He built it with Dad.

Plank by plank.

Nail by nail.

It sat high in the big oak tree.

It had a wooden floor.

It had two small windows.

It had a swaying rope ladder.

Benny smiled up at it.

"This is my treehouse," he said proudly.

On Saturday, he climbed up.

Up.

Up.

Up the ladder.

He sat in the corner with his book bag.

He reached inside.

No book.

"My book is not in Benny's treehouse," he said.

It was on the kitchen table.

Down he went.

Down.

Down.

Down the ladder.

He ran inside.

He grabbed his book.

Up he went again.

Up.

Up.

Up.

He sat down.

Then he blinked.

No water bottle.

"My water is not in Benny's treehouse," he said.

Down he went again.

Down.

Down.

Down.

He grabbed his bottle.

Up he went again.

Up.

Up.

Up.

Now he had his book.

Now he had his water.

Benny looked around.

The treehouse felt quiet and cozy.

A brown leaf had blown in.

Two tiny acorns rolled in the corner.

Benny smiled.

"This is the best place," he said.

He opened his book.

He read and read.

The sun moved across the sky.

The treehouse stayed strong and steady.

When Mom called him for supper, Benny climbed down slowly.

He looked back at the oak tree.

"My treehouse will be here tomorrow," he said.

And he could not wait to climb up again.

Spanish

CUENTO 11: LA CASA-ÁRBOL DE BENNY

Benny amaba su casa-árbol.

La había construido con su papá.

Tablón por tablón.

Clavo por clavo.

Descansaba en lo alto del gran roble.

Tenía piso de madera.

Tenía dos pequeñas ventanas.

Tenía una escalera de cuerda bamboleante.

Benny sonrió al verla.

—Esta es mi casa-árbol —dijo con orgullo.

Subió el sábado.

Subió.

Subió.

Subió la escalera.

Se sentó en una esquina con su mochila escolar.

Introdujo la mano.

Su libro no estaba.

—Mi libro no está en la casa-árbol de Benny —se dijo a sí mismo.

Lo había dejado en la mesa de la cocina.

Debía bajar.

Bajó.

Bajó.

Bajó las escaleras.

Entró corriendo.

Tomó su libro.

Volvió a subir.

Subió.

Subió.

Subió.

Se sentó.

Pestañeó.

No tenía su botella de agua.

—Mi botella de agua no está en la casa-árbol de Benny —se dijo a sí mismo.

Volvió a bajar.

Bajó.

Bajó.

Bajó.

Tomó su botella de agua.

Volvió a subir.

Subió.

Subió.

Subió.

Esta vez tenía su libro.

Esta vez tenía su botella de agua.

Benny miró a su alrededor.

La casa-árbol era silenciosa y acogedora.

Entró una hoja marrón.

Dos bellotas rodaron hacia la esquina.

Benny sonrió.

—Este es el mejor lugar —dijo.

Abrió su libro.

Leyó y continuó leyendo.

El sol siguió su camino a través del cielo.

La casa-árbol permaneció fuerte y firme.

Cuando su mamá lo llamó para cenar, Benny bajó lentamente.

Volteó a ver el roble.

—Mi casa-árbol estará aquí mañana —dijo.

No podía esperar para volver a escalar su casa-árbol.

Vocabulary

Illustration	English	Español
	TREEHOUSE	CASA-ÁRBOL
	PLANK	TABLÓN
	LEAF	HOJA
	ACORN	BELLOTA

Your Turn

Illustration	English	Español
	T _ _ _ _ _ _ _ E	C _ _ _ _ _ _ _ L

Illustration	English	Español
	P _ _ _ K	T_ _ _ _ N
	L _ _ F	H_ _A
	A _ _ _ N	B_ _ _ _ _ TA

STORY 12

My Red Ball

English

I love my red ball.

It is bright.

It is round.

It is bouncy.

My red ball is the best.

On Saturday, I took my red ball to the park.

I bounced it on the path.

Bounce.

Bounce.

Bounce.

I kicked it across the grass.

Roll.

Roll.

Roll.

Then I threw it up high.

Up.

Up.

Up.

But when it came down,

It did not land in my hands.

It rolled away.

My red ball rolled fast.

It rolled past the bench.

It rolled past the slide.

It rolled toward the hill.

"Oh no," I said.

"My red ball!"

I ran after it.

Step.

Step.

Step.

My red ball kept rolling.

"I can catch it," I said.

"I can catch my red ball."

It rolled down the hill.

It bumped a rock.

Bonk!

It changed direction.

It rolled toward the sandbox.

I ran faster.

"I can catch it," I said again.

Just before it reached the fence,

I grabbed it.

I held my red ball tight against my chest.

I laughed.

"My red ball," I said.

It was still bright.

It was still round.

It was still bouncy.

I bounced it again.

Bounce.

Bounce.

Bounce.

This time, I kept my eyes on it.

My red ball stayed with me all afternoon.

And when it was time to go home,

I carried my red ball under my arm.

Because my red ball is the best ball.

Spanish

CUENTO 12: MI PELOTA ROJA

Amo mi pelota roja.

Su color es vivo.

Es redonda.

Rebota.

Mi pelota roja es la mejor.

El sábado llevé mi pelota roja al parque.

La hice rebotar en el camino.

Rebotó.

Rebotó.

Rebotó.

La pateé hacia el otro lado del césped.

Rodó.

Rodó.

Rodó.

La lancé hacia arriba muy alto.

Arriba.

Arriba.

Arriba.

Pero cuando bajó,

no cayó en mis manos.

Siguió rodando.

Mi pelota roja rodó rápido.

Rodó hasta pasar el banco.

Rodó hasta pasar el tobogán.

Rodó hasta la colina.

—Oh no —exclamé.

—¡Mi pelota roja!

Corrí tras ella.

Paso.

Paso.

Paso.

Mi pelota roja siguió rodando.

—La puedo alcanzar —me dije a mí mismo.

—Puedo alcanzar mi pelota roja.

Bajó cuesta abajo.

Chocó contra una roca.

¡Pumba!

Cambió de dirección.

Rodó hacia el arenero.

Corrí más rápido.

—La puedo alcanzar —me repetí.

Antes de que llegara al cerco,

la alcancé.

Apreté mi pelota roja contra mi pecho.

Reí.

—Mi pelota roja —dije.

Seguía siendo de un color vivo.

Seguía siendo redonda.

Seguía rebotando.

La hice rebotar nuevamente.

Rebotó.

Rebotó.

Rebotó.

Pero esta vez no le quité los ojos de encima.

Mi pelota roja estuvo conmigo toda la tarde.

Cuando llegó la hora de ir a casa,

llevé mi pelota roja bajo el brazo.

Porque mi pelota roja es la mejor pelota.

Vocabulary

Illustration	English	Español
	BALL	PELOTA

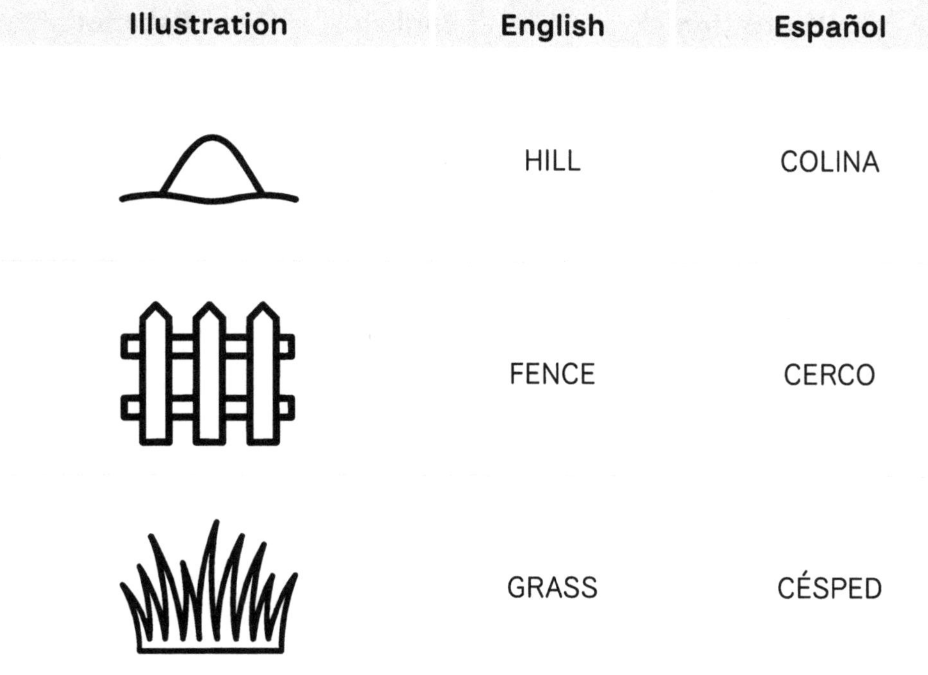

Illustration	English	Español
	HILL	COLINA
	FENCE	CERCO
	GRASS	CÉSPED

Your Turn

Illustration	English	Español
	B _ _ L	P _ _ _ _A
	H _ _ L	C _ _ _ _A
	F _ _ _ _ E	C_ _ _ O

Illustration	English	Español
	G _ _ _ S	C_ _ _ _D

A Note Before You Close the Book

You made it to the last page. So did your child. Do not let that go unnoticed.

What happened between the first story and this one was not small. Your child sat with twelve different moments, twelve different children, and twelve different ways of getting through something hard. They watched Milo problem-solve in his garden. They cheered for Nadia at the swing. They took one small step forward with Sam at the pond. And then, in the final story, they stopped watching altogether and became the one running after the ball themselves. That was not an accident. That was the whole journey.

Every time you read one of these stories aloud, you were doing more than filling time before bed or before dinner. You were showing your child that sitting with a story is worth it. That finishing something matters. That the words on a page are meant for them. Those are not small lessons. Those are the ones that stay.

If your child now asks to read a story on their own, let them. If they want you to read it to them again, do that too. Both are wins. Both mean the same thing: a child who believes they belong in a story.

The Spanish side of this book gives you somewhere new to go when the English side feels familiar. Return to a favorite story and read it through in Spanish. You may be surprised how much your child already understands, because the story is already living in them. Language is just a new coat for something they already know.

Keep reading together for as long as they will let you. It goes faster than you think.

Change Lives with Your Review

Share the Gift of Reading

"One language sets you in a corridor for life. Two languages open every door along the way."
— Frank Smith, Psycholinguist

Parents who invest in their children's growth tend to raise more confident, curious, and connected kids. Let's team up to make a difference!

Can you lend a hand to someone just like you, a parent who wants the best for their child but is not sure where to start with bilingual reading?

My goal is to make raising a bilingual reader feel simple, joyful, and totally possible for every family.

To spread the word, I need your support.

Most parents choose books because of reviews from other parents. So I am asking you, a fellow family builder, to leave a quick and honest review.

It is free, takes less than a minute, and your honest words could change the direction of a child's life. If this book made a difference in your home, your honest words might...

- Give one more child the gift of two languages before they start school.
- Help one more parent feel confident reading with their child every night.
- Show one more family that 15 minutes a day is enough to make a real difference.
- Connect one more child to their culture, their heritage, and their voice.
- Turn one more bedtime story into a lifelong love of reading.

To help out, just scan the QR code below and drop a review:

[https://www.amazon.com/review/review-your-purchases/?asin=BOOKASIN]

If you believe every child deserves the chance to grow up hearing two languages, we are kindred spirits. Thank you so much from the bottom of my heart!

World Voice Bridge

www.ingramcontent.com/pod-product-compliance
Lightning Source LLC
LaVergne TN
LVHW081320110826
845149LV00006B/1557
9781972535004